HOW TO MAKE A SAAMI INSPIRED PEWTER
THREAD BRACELET

SAAMI INSPIRED
BRACELET BASICS
LIZ BUCHEIT

**MAKE THIS
BRACELET!**

Acknowledgements

I wish to dedicate this book as follows:
To my partner in all things, Michael Seiler, for his encouragement, vision and computer expertise.
To McKay Bram for her endless hours of documenting and creating various projects and sharing her processes on social media.
Also, special thanks to all of my students over the years for contributing to the legacy of Scandinavian craft.

E-book Development and Design: Michael Seiler
Photography: Michael Seiler and McKay Bram
Written by Liz Bucheit

Visit our website at: saamisupplies.com
Secure online ordering available

Table of contents

Chapter 1

Introduction

"Tradition is not the worship of ashes, but the preservation of fire."
-Gustav Mahler

Welcome to the wonderful world of pewter thread adornment!

I have always been fascinated and inspired by folk craft from around the world. The tradition of creating objects by hand is as old as mankind's existence. Our love and appreciation of beautiful objects functions as a universal language human beings share cross culturally. Historically, jewelry is one of the oldest and most portable forms of traveling art and craft still relevant today. We can tell a lot about the mobility of our ancestors over the ages by the type of jewelry and other various items they traded with local cultures around the world. During the Viking Age people used spun gold, silver and bronze thread as a type of embroidery for decorating their clothing and leather goods. Examples of spun gold thread have been found in Viking graves dating back 3,000 years. Examples of pewter (tin) thread found in Sweden dates back to around 1000 AD. In the 1600's the Saami culture of Scandinavia used tin thread embroidery to create beautiful patterns on reindeer hide and wool clothing. It is speculated they devised the method of spinning wire thread from trade with the Norwegians who brought tin from Ireland and England to local markets. Producing the tin thread consisted of melting metal and pouring the molten material into a hollowed out tree branch to create a stick form. The metal stick was then pulled through a series of holes in a reindeer horn drawplate down to a thin wire that was spun around a piece of reindeer sinew. Tin thread embroidery almost disappeared at the beginning of the 20th century but was rediscovered and revived by Andreas Wilks in Dikanas, Sweden in 1905. Thanks to his educational efforts in offering classes throughout Sweden he kept the craft alive.

For more information regarding tin thread embroidery I recommend <u>Tenntrads Broiderier</u> by Mona Callenberg. (This book is written in Swedish)

The beauty with many traditions is how techniques and materials are reinterpreted by the individual making the work. Tin thread embroidery is one of the traditional uses of spun thread. More recently tin thread "braiding" has become popular in the creation of bracelets and necklaces. The art of creating pewter thread jewelry is what I term a 'tradition in transition'. What makes this project "Saami inspired" is the use of culturally specific components regarding the use of tin thread, reindeer hide and antler buttons.

Chapter 2 - Materials

Materials

Tennetrad (48" cut in 3@ 16" sections) 0.35mm
20mm reindeer hide strip (6.75")
Reindeer leather twisted cord (2.25") for loop
5mm reindeer hide strip (2") for button
Reindeer antler two hole button
1@ 5/10 straight needle (to use with acrylic thread to fasten braid to leather)
1@ leather "glover" needle (to use with synthetic sinew to fasten button, loop and close up back of bracelet.
Acrylic ("invisible") thread
Synthetic sinew – waxed linen
Scissors
Measuring tape
Plastic hobby table clamp with hole(s) in handle
Paper clip
Rubber cement or crafting glue
Toothpicks

Visit our website at: saamisupplies.com
Secure online ordering available

Materials

Page 7 of 102

Chapter 3 - Making the tin thread braid

After you have organized your materials you are ready to begin! Clamp your table vise with the handle facing towards you and grab a standard paper clip. You can use plastic coated or metal paper clips of any size or color.

Open the paper clip so you have a hook on either end and attach it through the hole on the end of the clamp with one of the hook ends facing up.

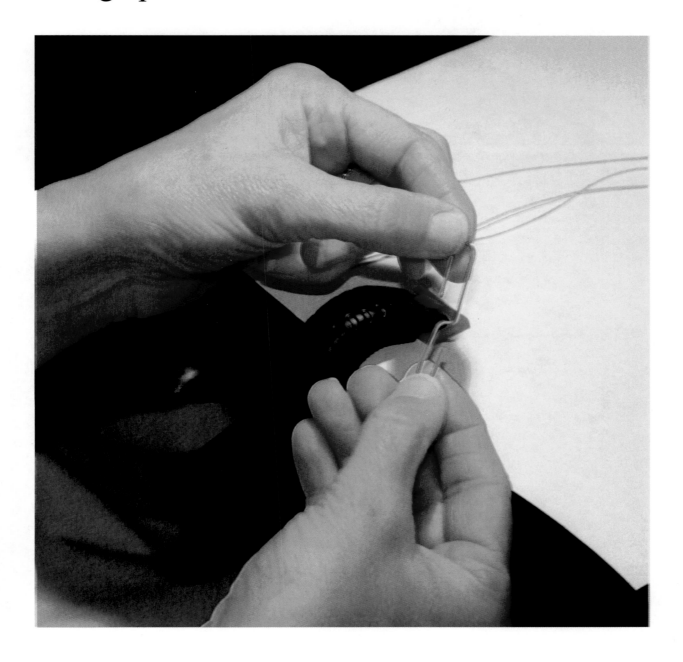

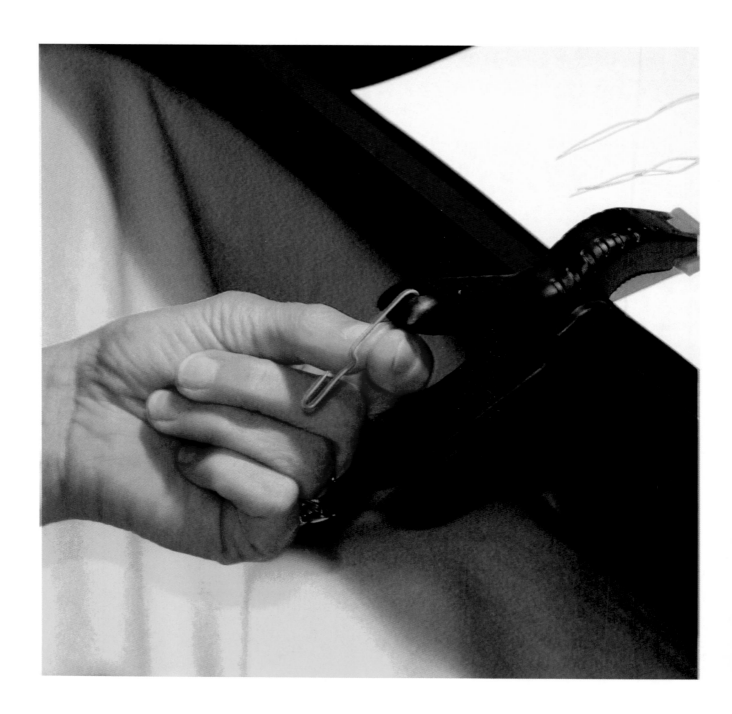

Take your three pieces of pewter thread and double it over off the end of the open hook of the paper clip. You may have to back your chair away from you table top in order to even up your strands. Maintain a light tension and pull the strands towards you.

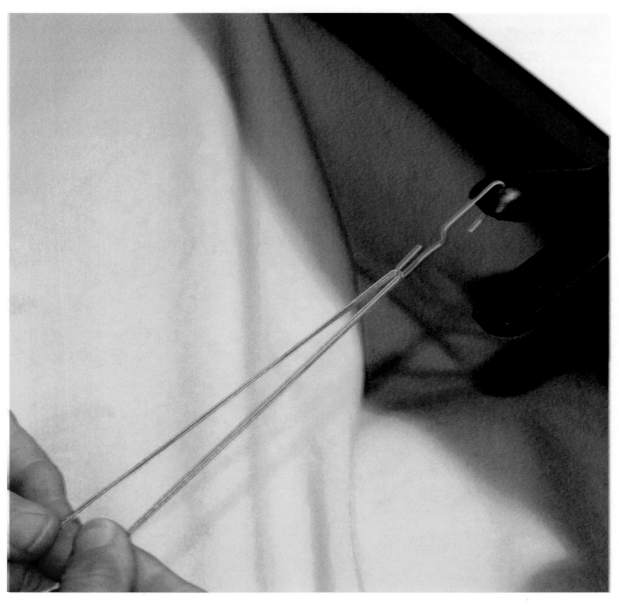

Divide your pewter thread into three sections with two strands in each section. Make sure your two strands in each section are right next to each other. Think of your sections as three pieces of flat layered ribbon while you are braiding. Do not "roll" the sections as you braid. Everything should be flat.

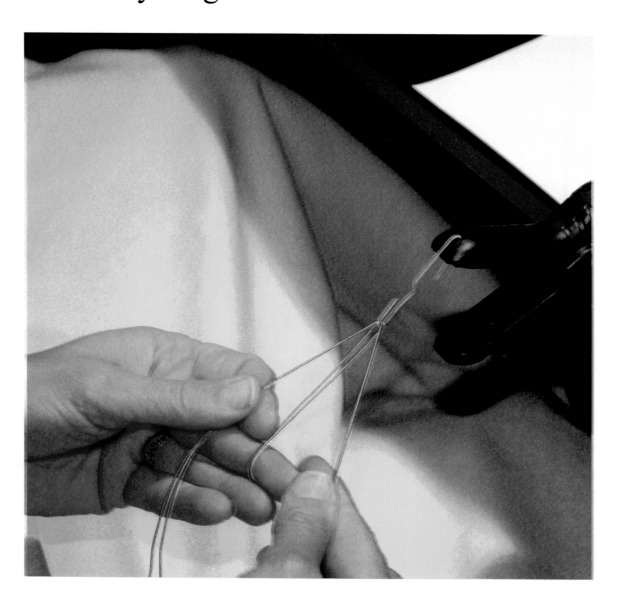

Here are a couple of tips to help you construct a consistent braid pattern! Keep in mind that when you start braiding the first 1/4" might not look consistent until you get going. Don't worry as part of the end of your braid will be concealed when your bracelet is finished. Use a bit of tension when you are braiding and pull the piece towards you. A tighter braid will appear to have more "heart" shape sections whereas a more loosely woven braid may look more V-shaped or herringbone in pattern.

Here are a series of photographs to help with the braiding process.

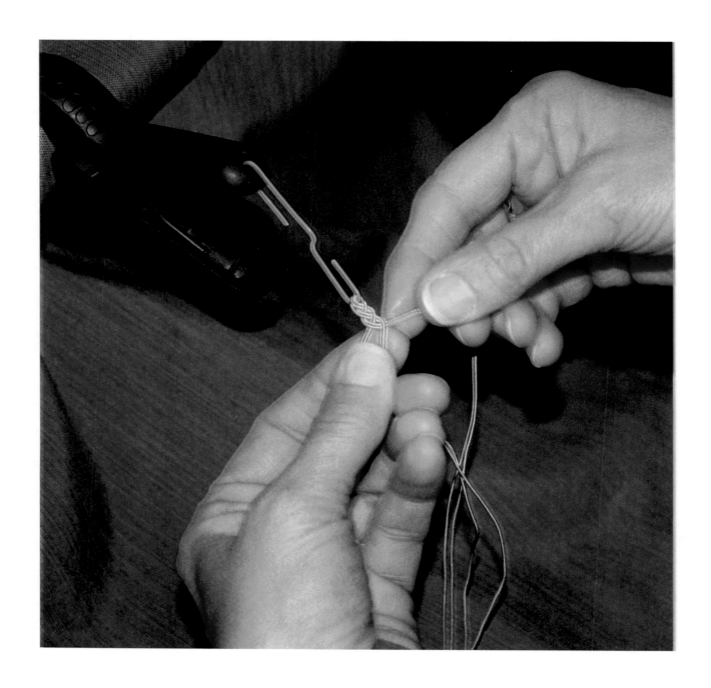

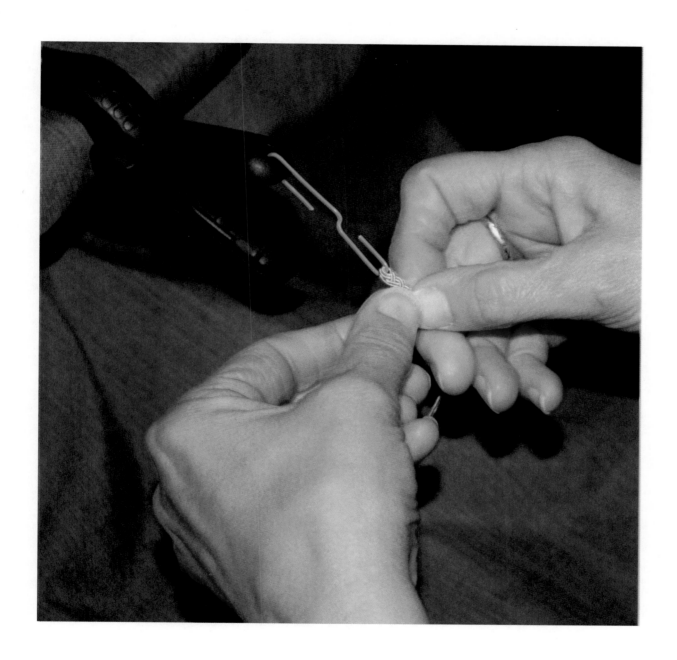

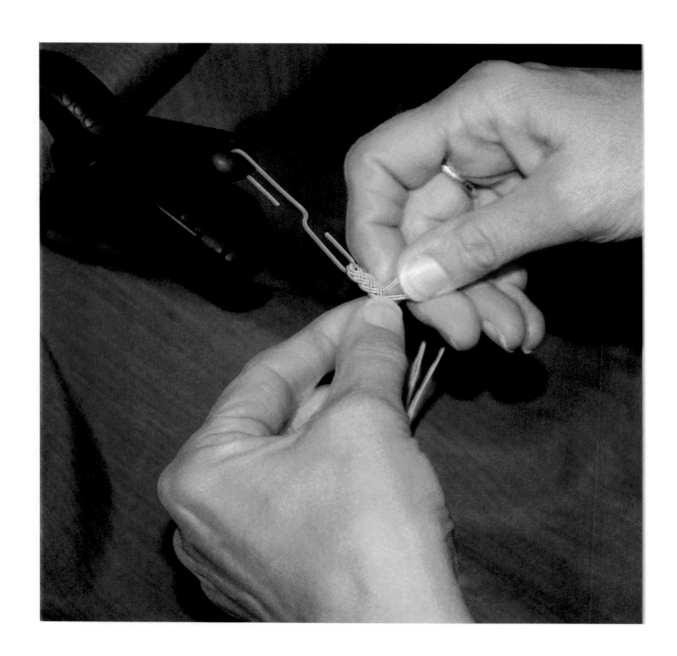

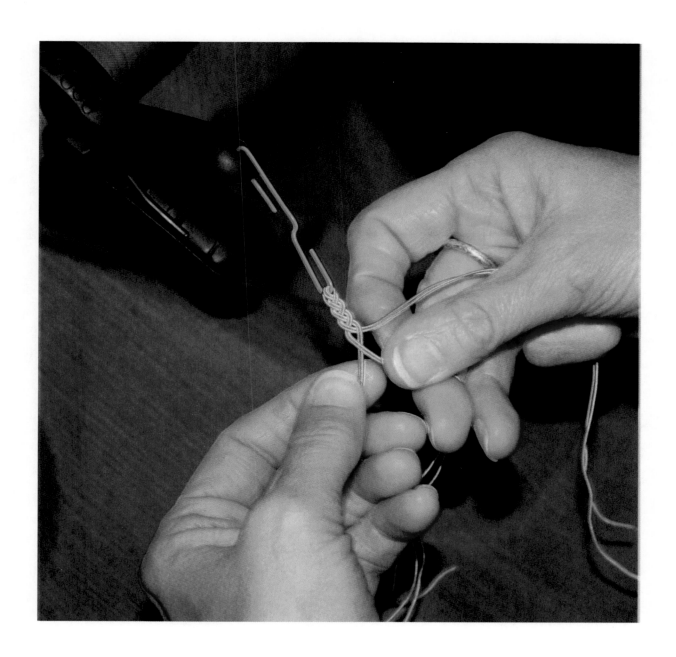

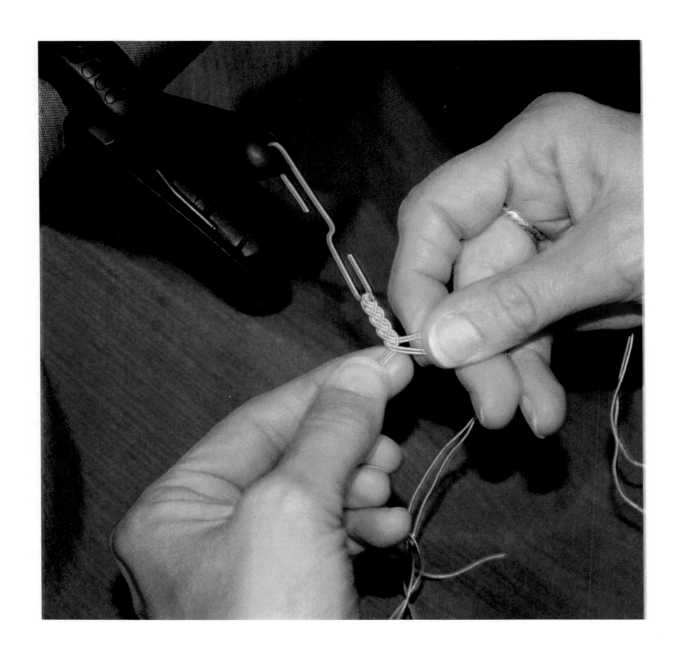

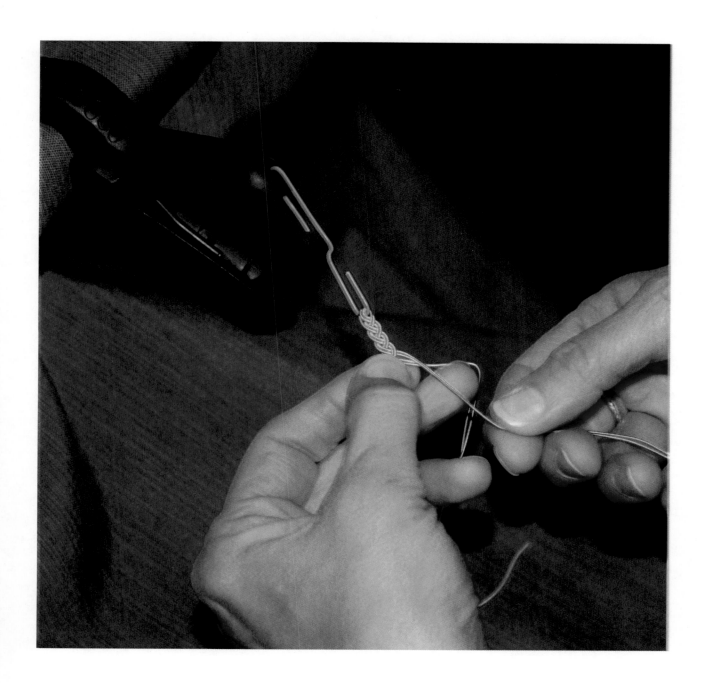

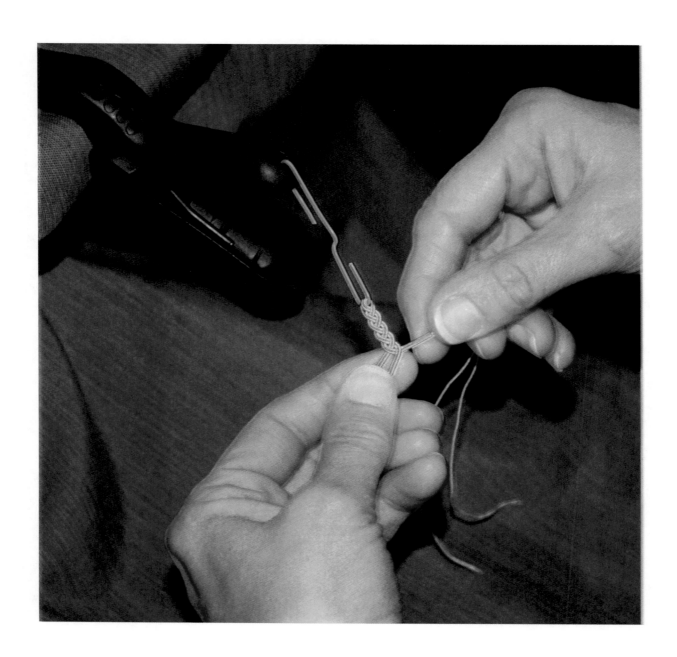

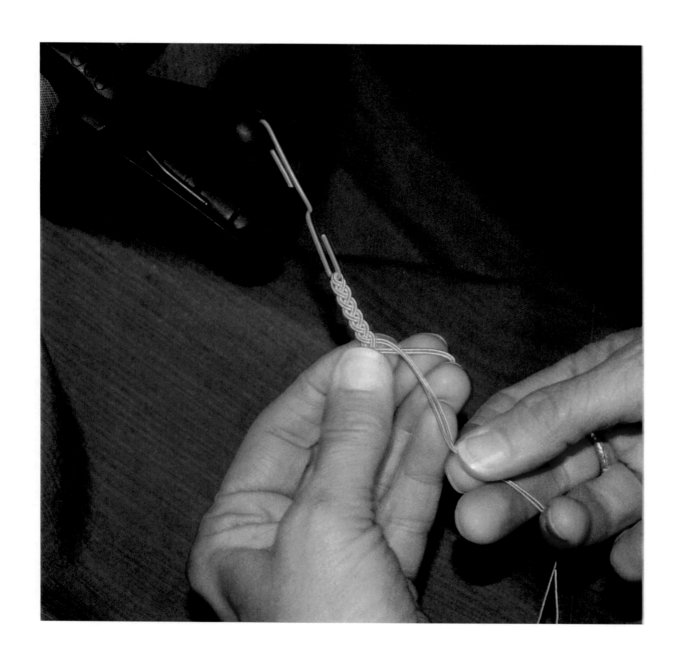

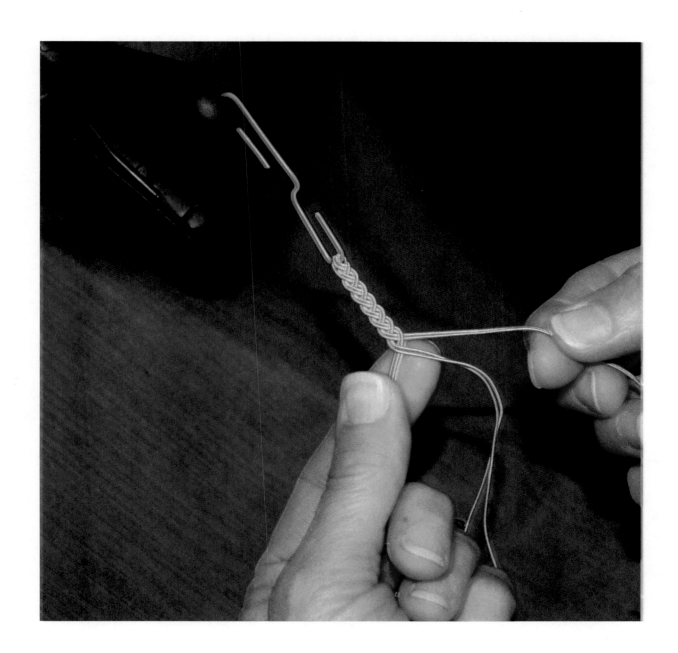

Complete your braid and leave about 1/2" of your remaining strands unbraided. Firmly grasp your braid and choose a pewter thread strand (doesn't matter which one) and using your thumbnail gently grab the end of the wire and gently uncoil. The white cotton core will be exposed. Unwrap the coil down to the body of your braid where your fingers are.

Click here for a video Link

If your the links don't work on your device go to
saamisupplies.com and see the learning page.

Using the uncoiled section of wire make a wrap around the end of your braid once or twice and trim all your strands (plus the exposed white cotton thread) evenly under the wrap leaving about a 1/4" length of fringe. You're now ready to attach your braid to the reindeer hide strip.

Chapter 4 - Laying out the reindeer leather

Lay your leather strip flat and measure 2cm from either edge towards the center of the bracelet and make a small mark or indentation with a white colored pencil, chalk or the point of your scissors. Center your braid on the strip between your marks and make sure you have at least 1/4" of braid extending past your marks towards the edge of your strip. If not, measure in a bit further (2.5 - 3cm) and make a small cut as pictured. This cut only needs to be as wide as your braid. It's best to make the cut smaller rather than bigger. If it's too small you can always go back in with your scissors and make it larger.

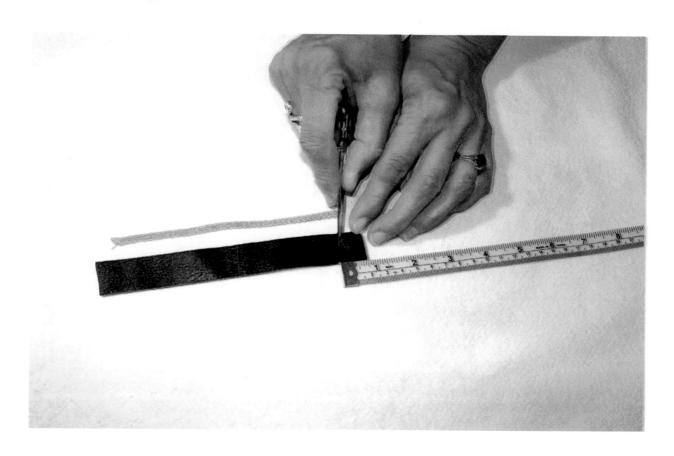

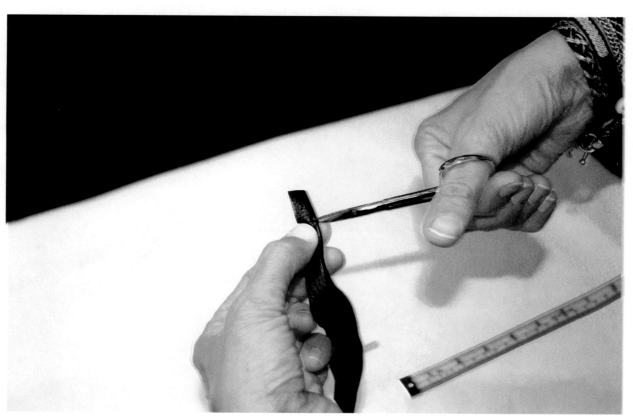

Feed the loop end of your braid through the cut on one end of the strip and swing it off to the side. Make sure to feed the braid from the sueded (back side) of the strip to the front (polished side) of the strip.

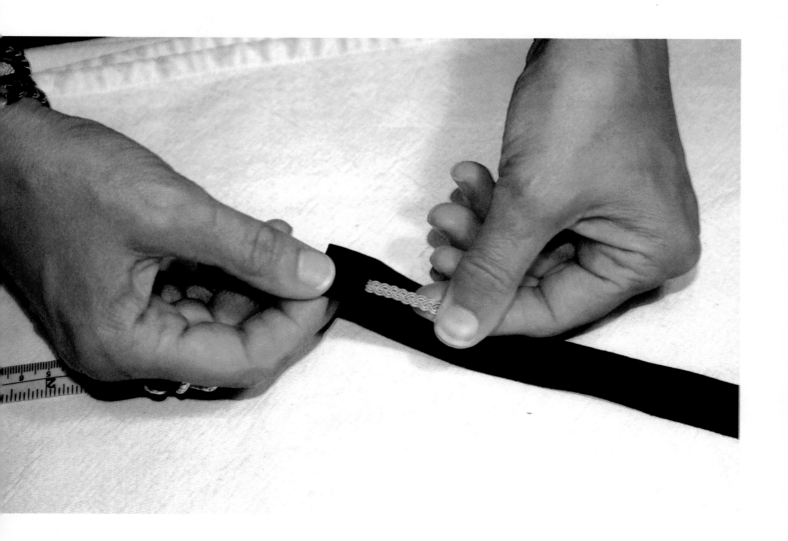

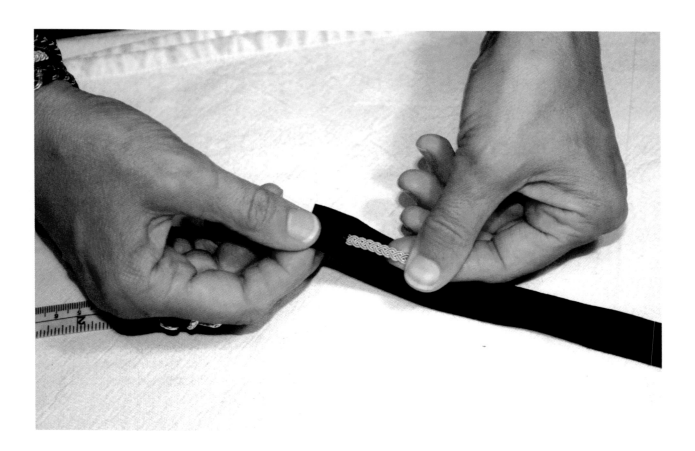

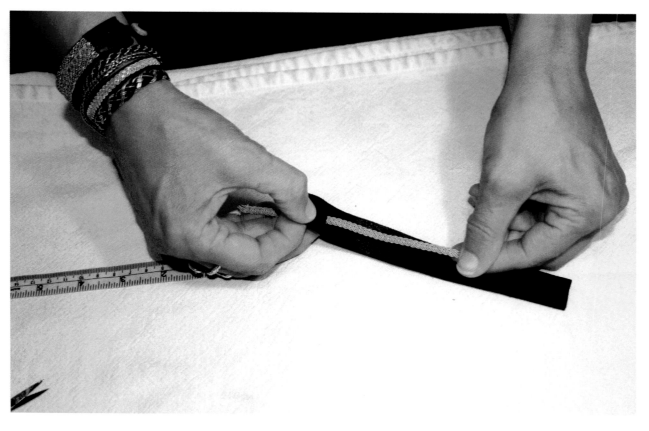

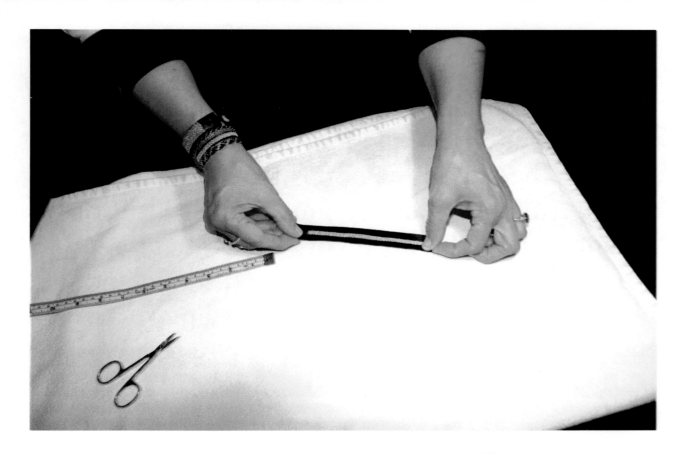

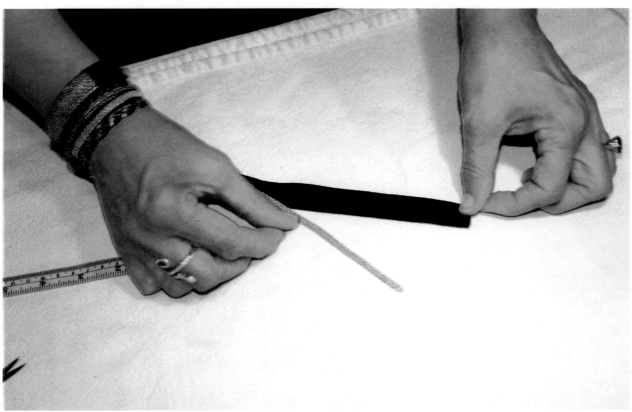

Apply a small bead of glue down the center of the strip and thread the loop end of your braid through the cut on the opposite end of the strip. Be careful not to use too much glue as it is only meant to help you keep your braid centered while you are sewing. Center your braid and clean up any extra glue with a toothpick. Give the glue a minute to dry and you are ready to start stitching!

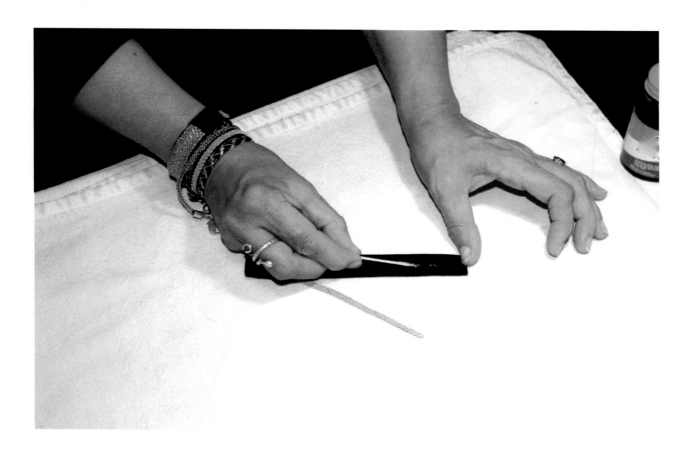

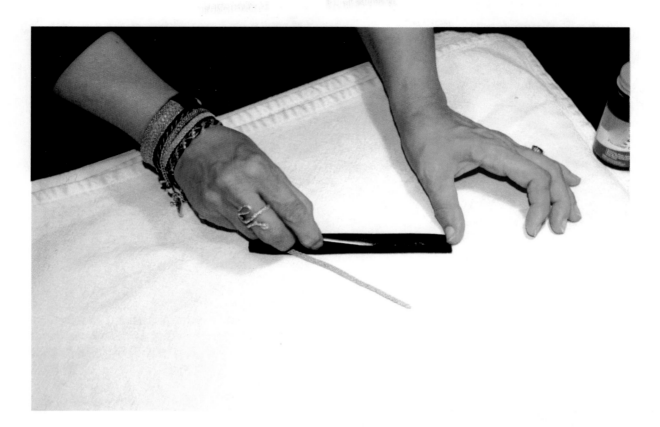

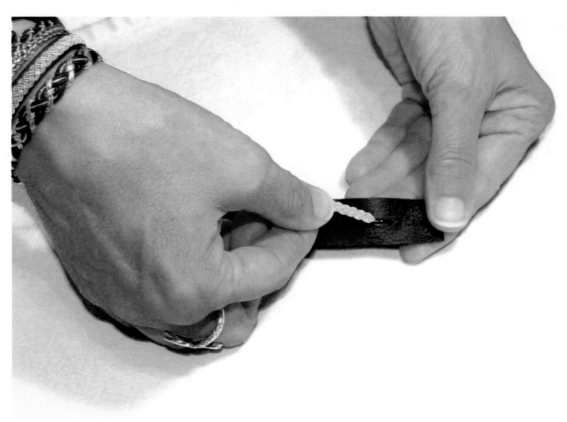

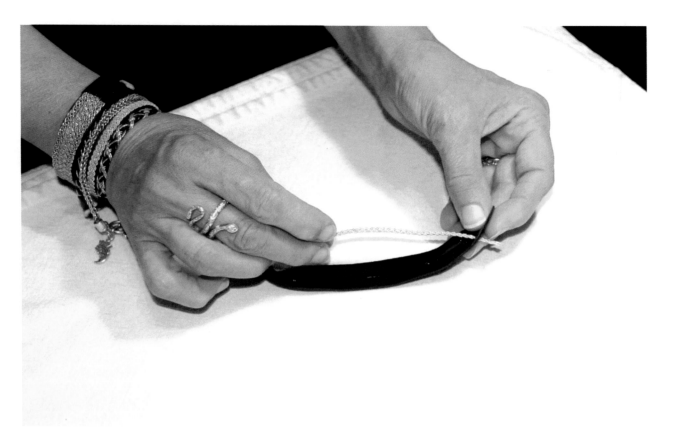

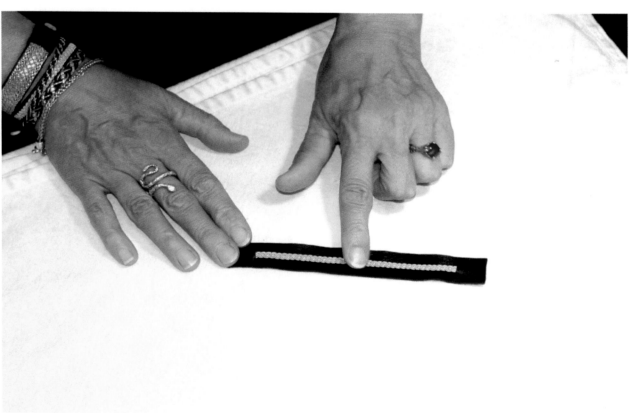

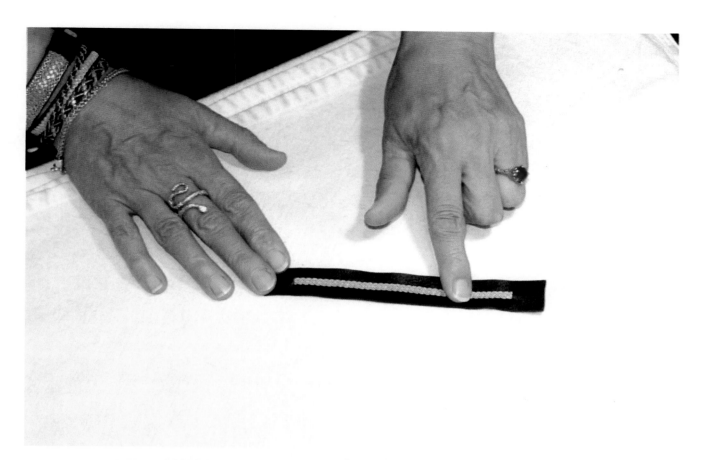

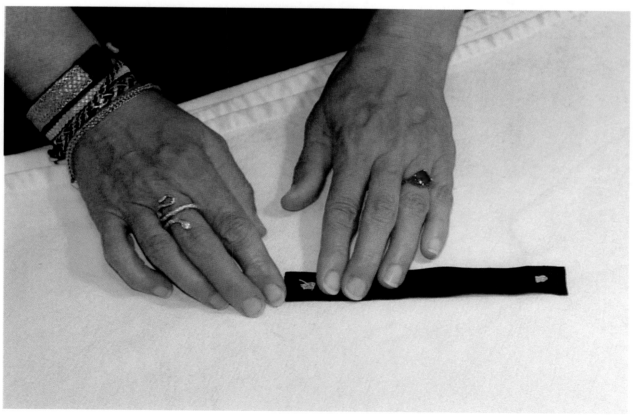

Chapter - 5 Attaching the tin thread braid

You are now ready to attach your braid to the leather strip using invisible thread and a thin embroidery needle. Cut an 18" section of invisible thread and thread your needle. You will need to tie a double knot right up to the eye of the needle leaving a 2-3" tail. This will prevent the thread from slipping out of the needle while you are sewing. (I love invisible thread for a lot of reasons but it's really slippery) Put a double knot in the other end of the thread and you're ready to go!

Starting from the back side (sueded) of the strip use your needle to pick up a small section of suede near the cut and pull your thread all the way through until your knot catches. This is what I call an "anchoring" stitch. We are not piecing the whole thickness of the strip just yet. If your thread pulls through and doesn't catch on your knot you'll need to make a bigger knot.

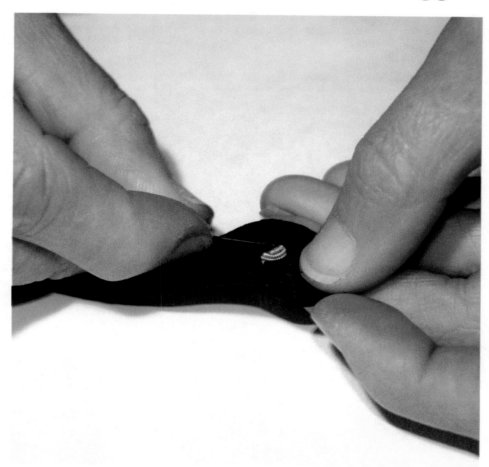

Next, feed your needle through the cut and pull the thread all the way through. Again, we aren't piercing the strip. Position your needle to the right or left side of braid. Make sure the braid is facing you as you get ready to make your first stitch.

Now, regardless of whether you chose to position your needle to the right or left of your braid, take your needle and crossing the two pewter thread strands on one side of the braid, pierce the hide and pull your thread all the way through to the back of your strip. The stitch you made will travel across the two pewter thread strands and enter the center of the braid where the sections cross.

Congratulations! You've made your first stitch. If you made your initial stitch on the right side of the braid you will need to come up on the opposite side of the braid with your needle to get ready to do another. Make sure your needle comes up super close to the outside edge of the braid so your stitches aren't visible.

In essence you will work right to left or left to right, stitching your way down the length of your braid in a zig -zag pattern. Make sure to pull your thread firmly (but not too tight) so the invisible thread disappears between the small coils of your pewter thread. Wherever the strands of your braid cross there should be a stitch. (diagram). Continue sewing the entire length of braid with the invisible thread, adding more if needed. To finish, make a knot on the back side (sueded) of the bracelet by picking up a bit of suede and making a small slip knot or loop. Any method of knotting will do provided it holds. Trim invisible thread by leaving a small tail after knotting. Trimming too close to the finished knot can cause it to come undone. (Ahh, I love invisible thread!)

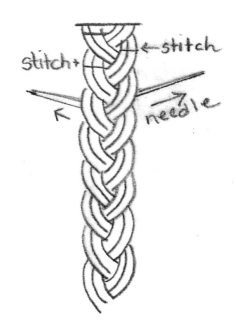

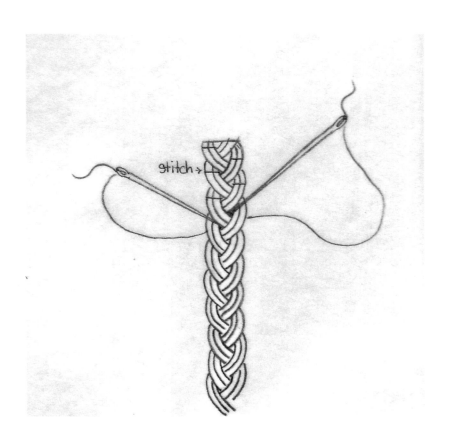

Chapter - 6 Adding a loop and button

The next few steps are very important regarding the durability of your bracelet. I have made revisions to the techniques of adding the loop and button closures after years of repairing bracelets that came apart at the clasp point. To begin, cut a 22-24" length of black cotton/poly thread or synthetic sinew (waxed linen thread) and thread your "glover" (leather needle). Make a knot at one end (you do not need to make a knot at the eye of the needle like you did with the transparent thread). *Do not "double the thread". We only need a single strand for sewing at this point. If you double the thread you will run out halfway through your sewing.

Taking your length of reindeer cord, fold it in half over your antler button. The button should be positioned sideways. We're trying to determine how wide the loop should be in order to feed the button through when the bracelet is clasped. This takes a bit of eye balling and it's better to make a loop that's a bit tighter than too loose. Remember, the loop with stretch and soften over time and wear. Next, take your needle and pierce in between the coils and pull the thread through to your knot. Wrap the thread around twice and on the third rotation pull the needle through the loop to form a slip knot and pull tight.

* Keep in mind there are a variety of ways to sew the loop to the strip. This example is very basic but many of my students have come up with alternatives that work just as well! Whatever you do, your loop and button have to hold or your bracelet will come apart. Trust your instincts and make sure both ends are strongly secured.

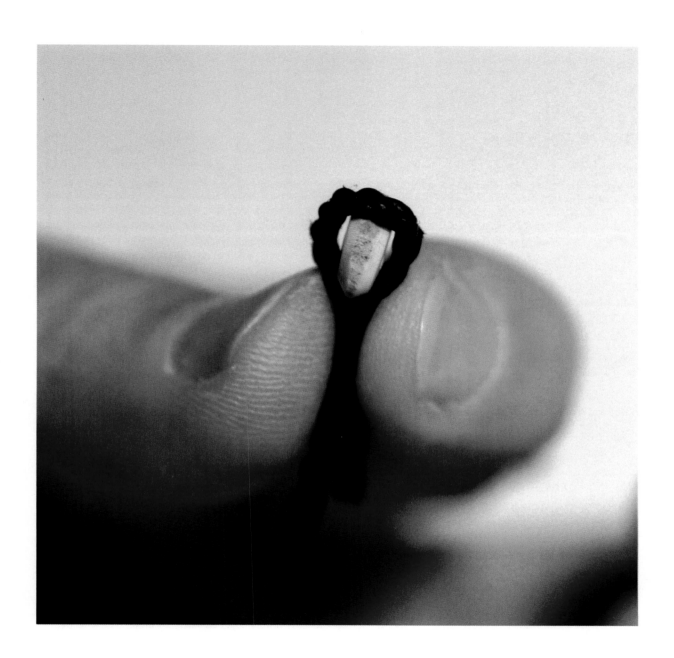

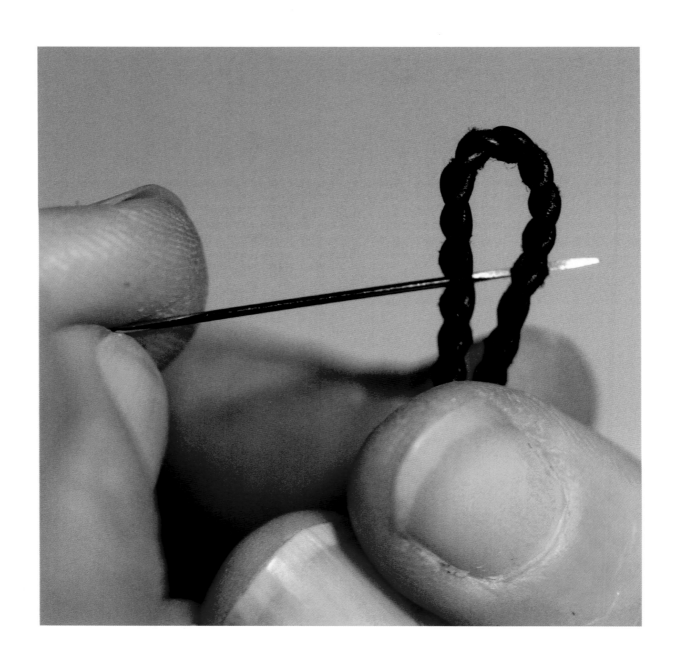

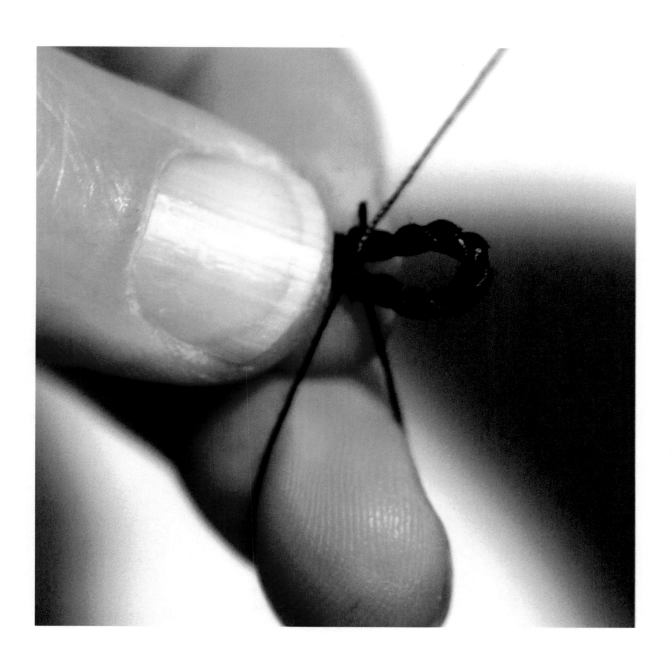

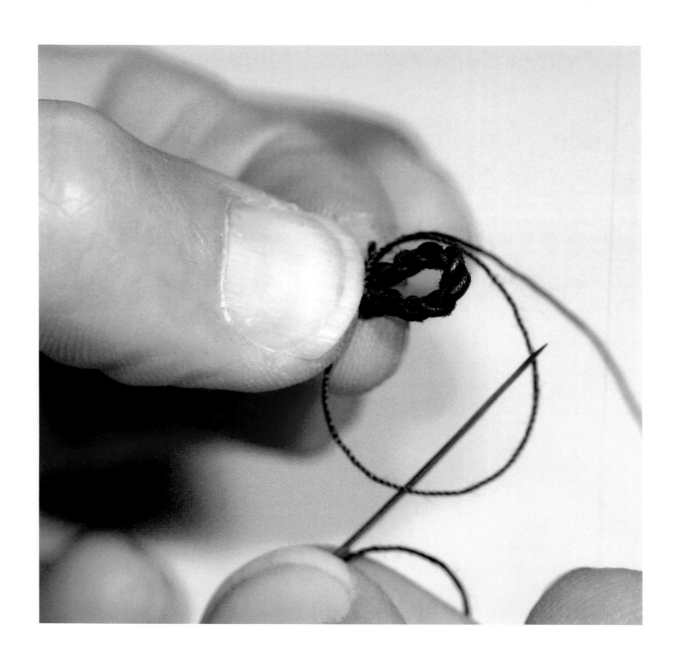

Chapter 7 -Anchoring the loop

Working from the back side of the leather strip, anchor the loop by threading the needle through the 3-loop end of your braid. Pull your thread through and position your loop off to the side of the leather strip. This is going to look loosey goosey but don't worry!

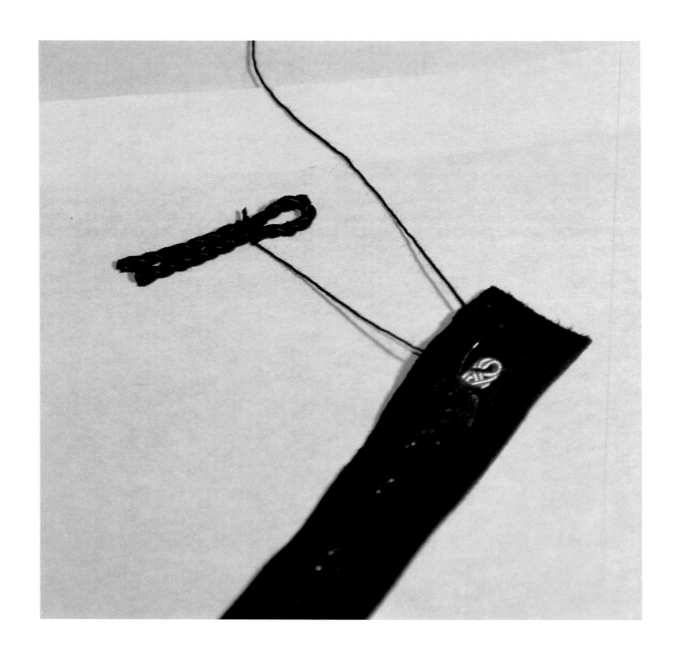

Using rubber cement or water soluble craft glue apply a thin coat of glue to the sueded side of the leather strip. Let the adhesive dry for a moment. Pull your needle and thread and center your loop on the edge of the bracelet. Make sure the wrap on the loop is below the edge of the strip. We don't want to see it peeking out! Apply glue only down to the cut at the bottom of your strip. (Fringe end) Leave the end open for the button.

You'll have a long length of thread once your loop is centered. At this point take your needle and push it through the upper left hand corner of the leather strip. Put a dab of glue on the "legs" of the loop and press the edges of the strip together and press them flat.

If the glue has dried and isn't sticking you can apply a little more.

It will feel awkward but be sure to hold the bracelet in your two hands while you are pressing the edges towards each other. The edges should just meet and not overlap. If you try pressing the edges together by pressing your piece down on a flat surface you can flatten the pewter thread. If pressing down on the piece is easier for you make sure to use a soft surface like a cloth or magazine to support the bracelet while you press the edges together.

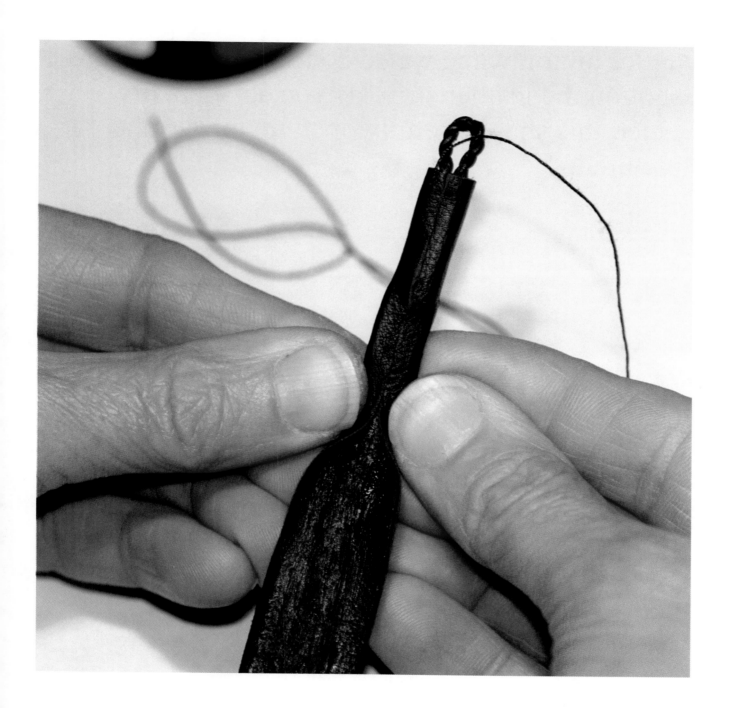

Remember to leave the opposite end of the bracelet open. We'll need to attach the reindeer antler button when we're done sewing the seam shut on the leather strip. If you accidentally glued this shut, carefully open up the strip as pictured.

As I mentioned before I've learned over years of repair work what might be improved regarding reinforcing and strengthening the loop and button closures on these bracelets. Working from the back side of the bracelet feed your needle through the loop and turn your bracelet so the pewter braid is facing you. Make a stitch about 1/4" from the edge of the bracelet and feed your needle so it exits between the legs of your loop underneath the wrap you made around the loop. Repeat. Essentially you are making a "cross" type stitch which goes over the wrap of your loop in the body of the strip.

Backside

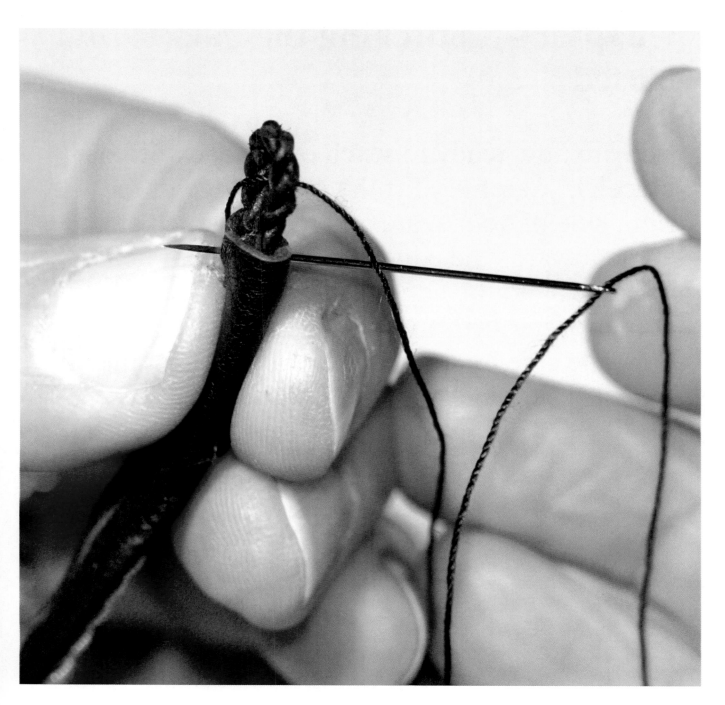

Sideview

Chapter - 8 Stitching the back closed

You are now ready to stitch of the back of your bracelet. Carefully lift the inside edge of the right side of your seam and make a stitch at an angle towards the edge. Don't exit your needle all the way to the edge- just grab the small corner of the strip for now. Repeat on the opposite side by turning the bracelet with the loop at 12 o'clock.

Once you have secured the left hand corner you will close the seam shut using longer stitches. Again, carefully lift the edge and make an angled stitch almost to the edge of the bracelet but not quite! Space your stitches evenly, about 1/8" apart. You can also space them little further apart too. It's important that the stitches aren't too close together or the thread starts to chew up the leather....better to err on the side of spacing your stitches farther apart. Continue sewing by working right to left (or left to right) by turning the bracelet to achieve "V" shaped stitches. This is similar to a herringbone embroidery stitch or what my mother would call a "bird foot" shape. Pull the thread in the direction of the "V" and you'll find the seam will want to come together,

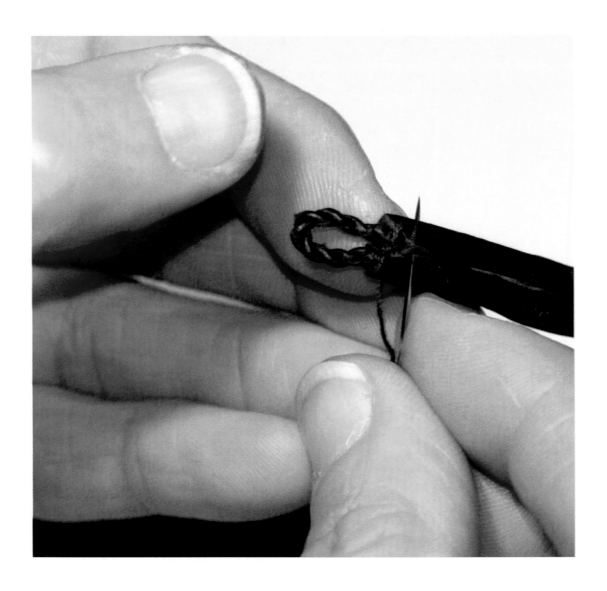

creating a nice pillowy pattern. Only sew down to the opening at the end of your bracelet.

*Be careful to lift the edge of your seam before making a stitch. You can break your invisible thread stitches if you dig your needle down too deep!

Click here for a video Link

If your the links don't work on your device go to
saamisupplies.com and see the learning page.

Button it up!
You're almost done! Using a thin strip of
leather (approximately 2" long and 1/4" wide)
cut one end at an angle to create a "needle"
shape.

Good quality antler buttons have a flat side and a domed side so the loop slides over the button easily when you are working the clasp. For this style of bracelet I use a 9-11 mm button. Feed the needle end of the leather strip from the flat underside of the button up through the button holes making sure the polished side of the leather is showing on top of the button.

Dab a small amount of glue on the sueded sections of your leather strip and press together.

Fold the remaining open end of your bracelet lengthwise and make a small cut (about 1/4" from the open edge of the leather) using the tips of your scissors and feed the button tabs through the opening. Pull the tabs until your button is flush with the surface of the leather.

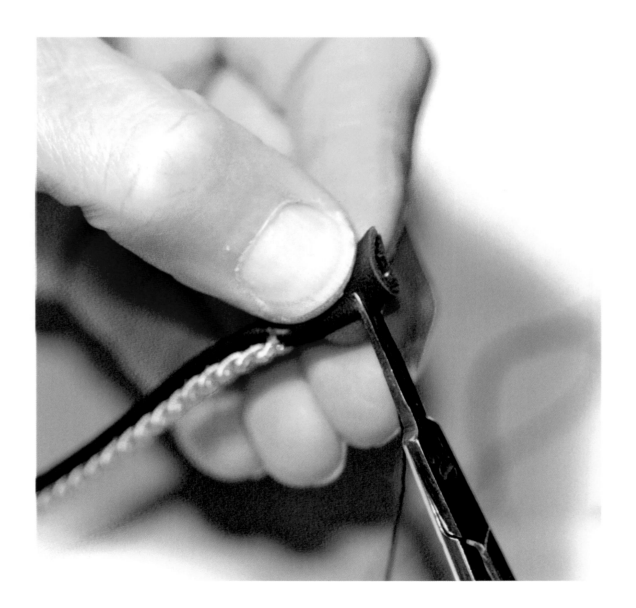

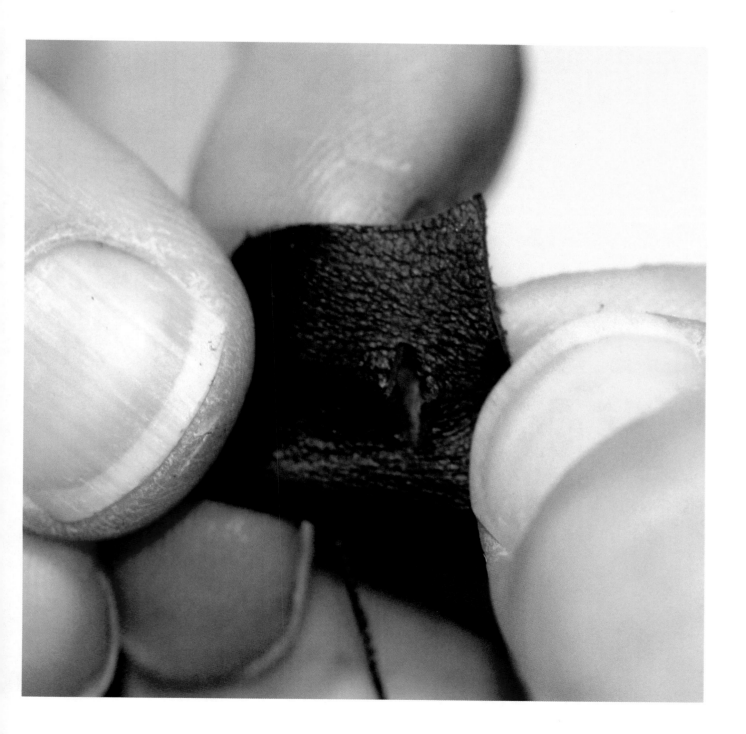

Apply a small amount of glue to the underside and top portion of your button tab and press your remaining seams together.

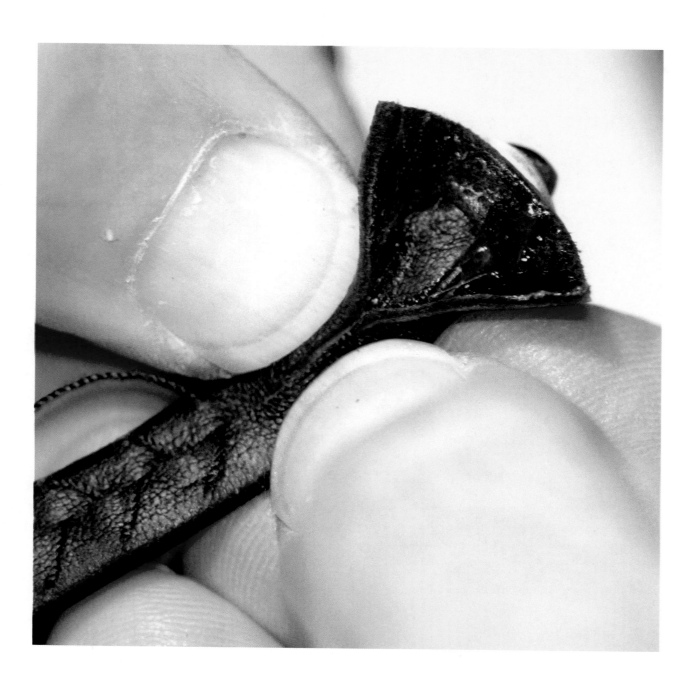

Continue stitching up to the point where you feel the button tab in the center of the bracelet. When you make your next few stitches drive your needle deep enough into the center of the bracelet so you catch a portion of the tab in your exiting stitch. Repeat this step (you'll probably get a good 2-3 deep stitches) until you are at the end of your strip. *This is important! If you don't grab some of the button tab leather in your stitches the button will just pull out when you go to fasten your bracelet.

Stitch down to the end of the strip. Take your needle and drive it through the center seam from the back and angle it so it comes up underneath the button. In addition to capturing the tabs attached to your button by your previous stitches, you have also made a stitch through your button tab within the interior of the bracelet. This step reinforces the strength of your closure over many fastenings!

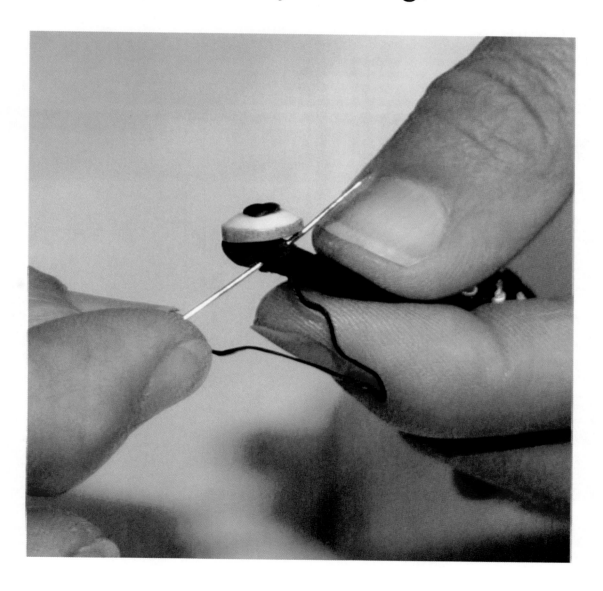

Next, wrap the thread several times around the underside of the button. If you've ever sewn a button on a coat this is the classic way to do it. Again, this step works to reinforce the strength of your closure. The wax on the synthetic sinew adds a bit of waterproofing and helps prevent premature wear and tear on the leather directly under the button. Feed the needle back down through the bracelet so it exits the center seam. You are now minutes away from completion! There are several options for finishing. I like to back the eye of the needle through the nearest stitch, make a slipknot and run the rest of the synthetic sinew down through the center seam. That way I can trim the remaining thread flush with the strip and I won't have a loose thread hanging out.

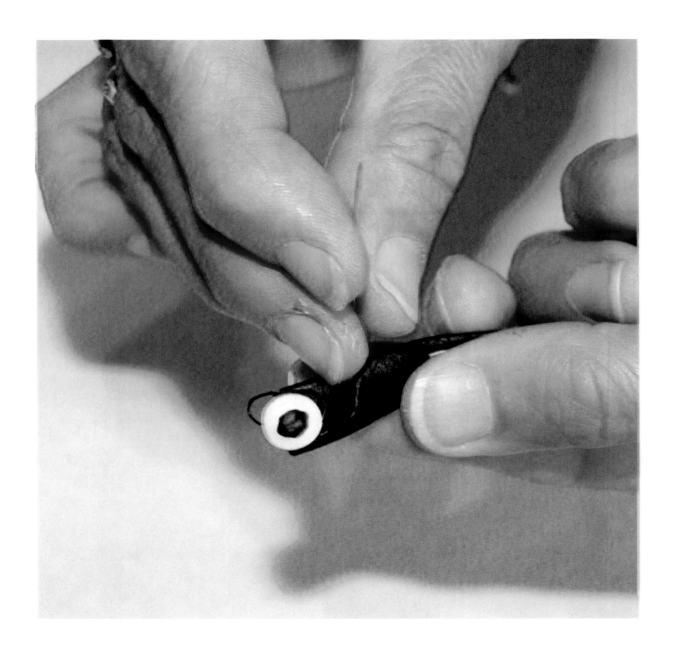

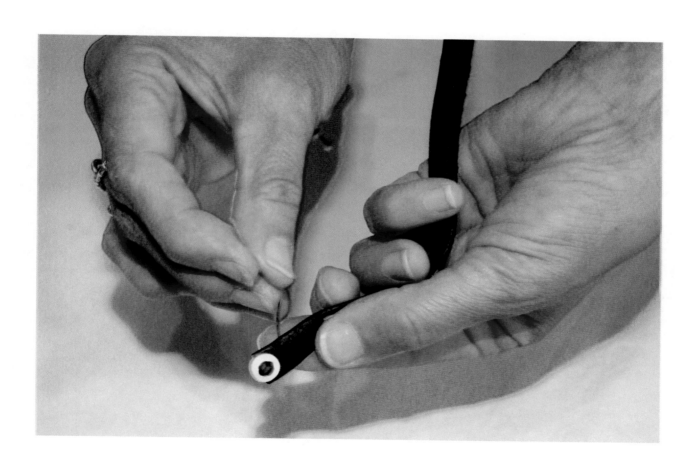

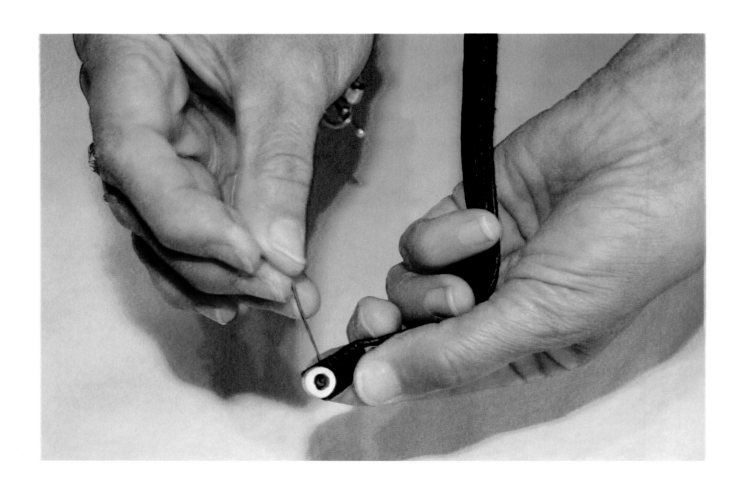

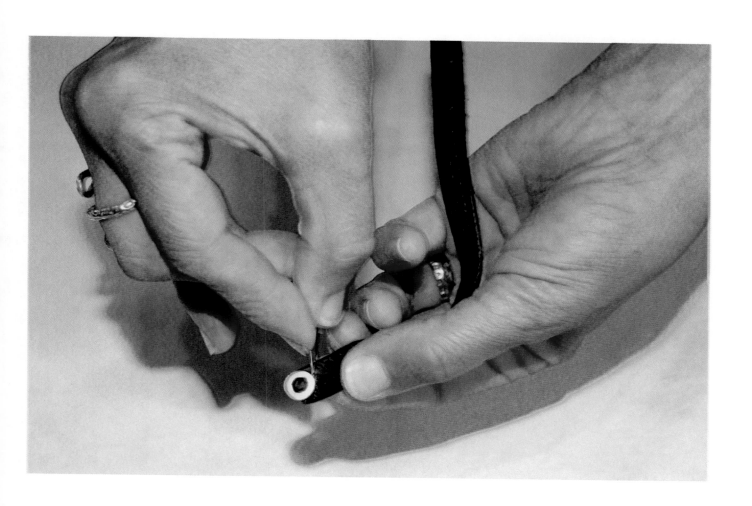

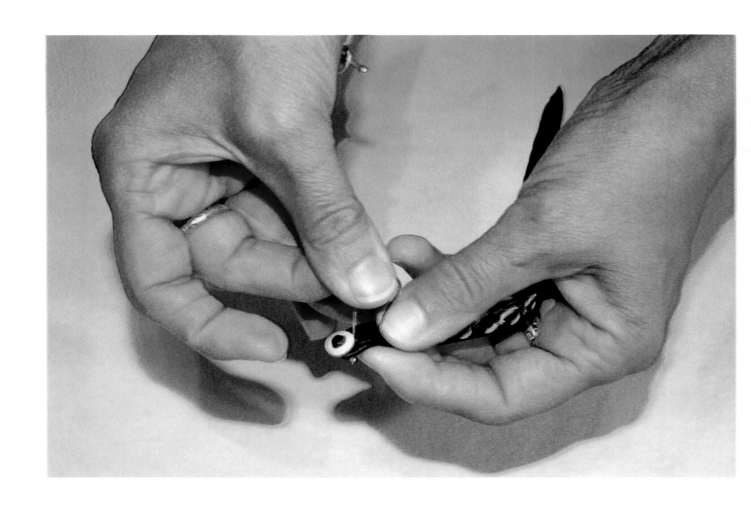

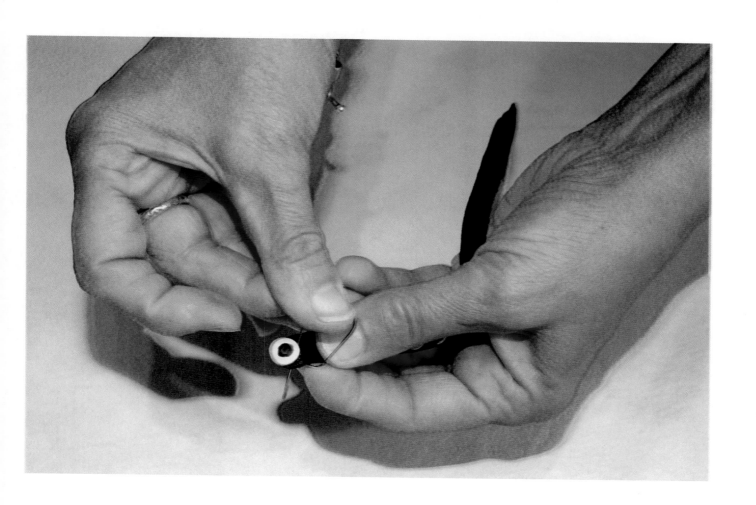

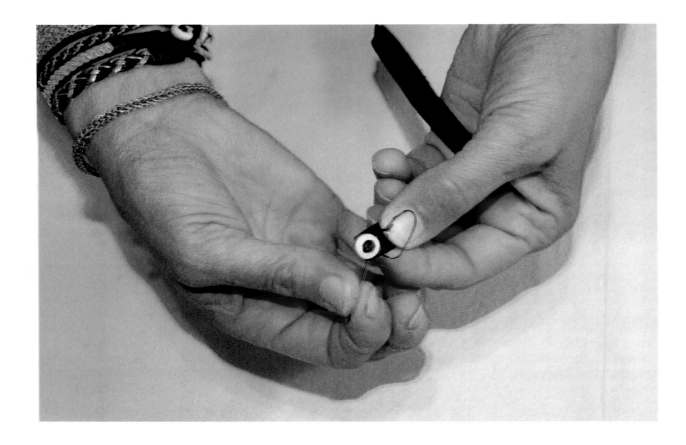

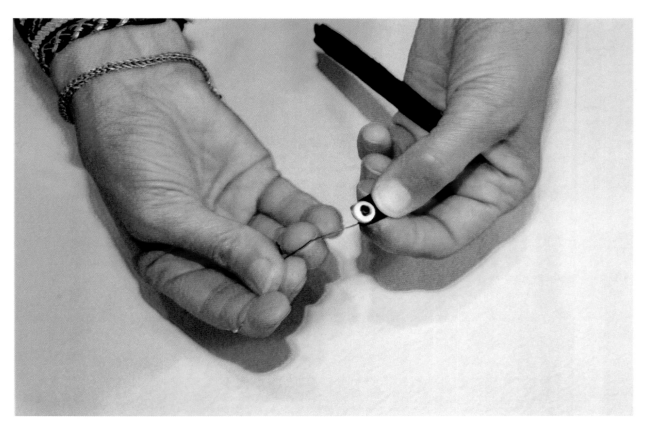

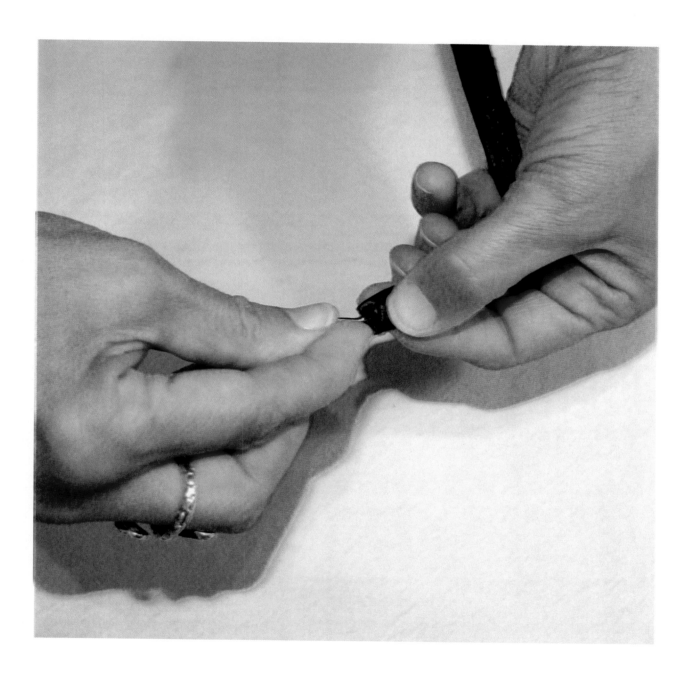

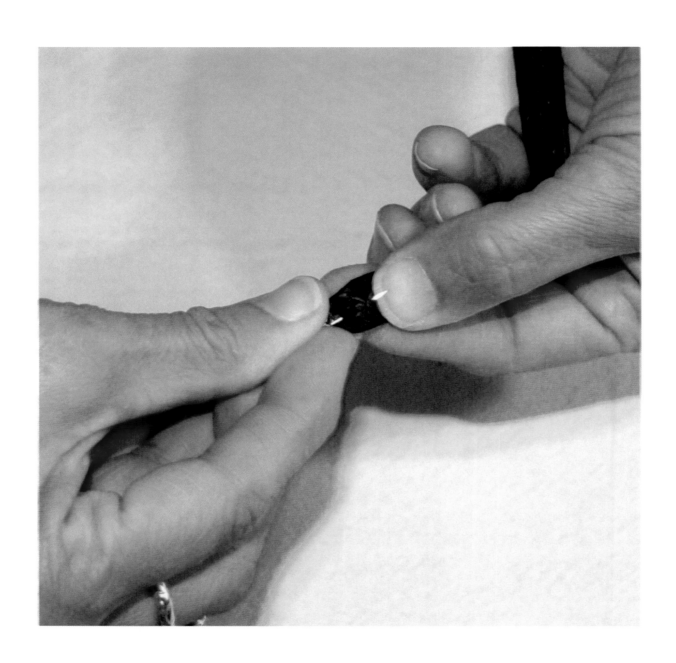

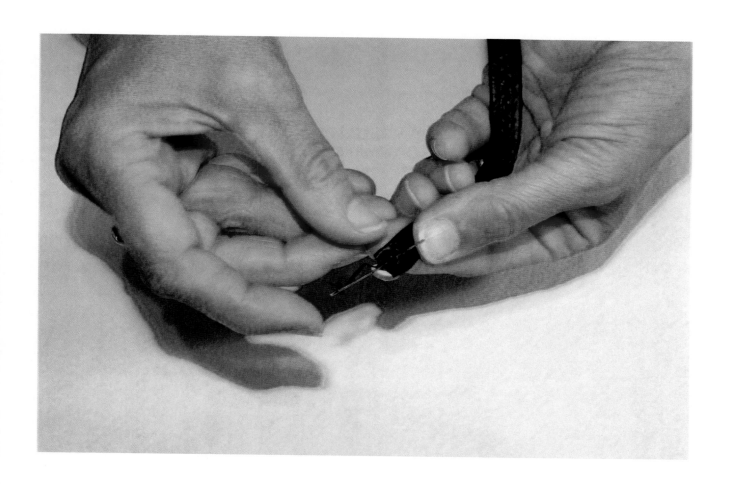

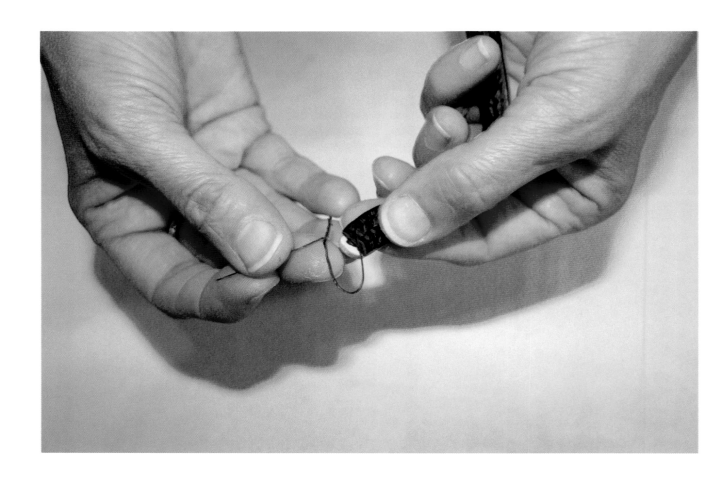

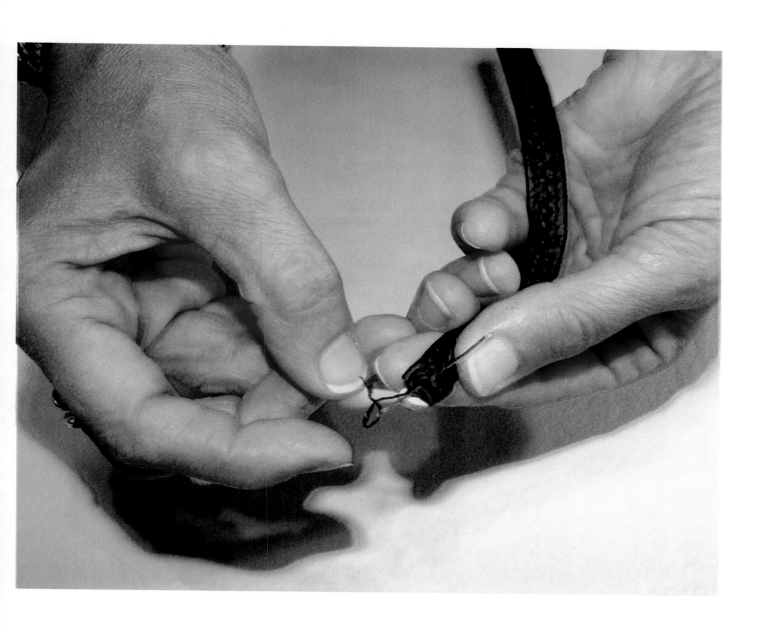

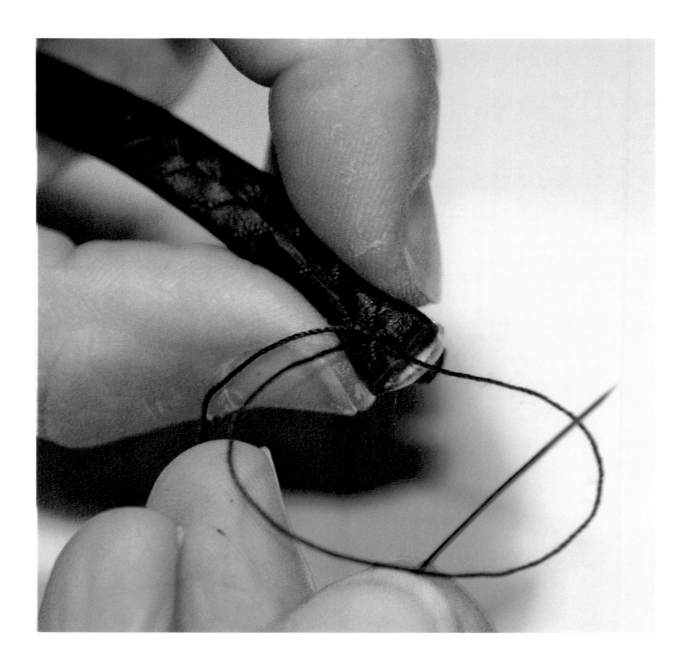

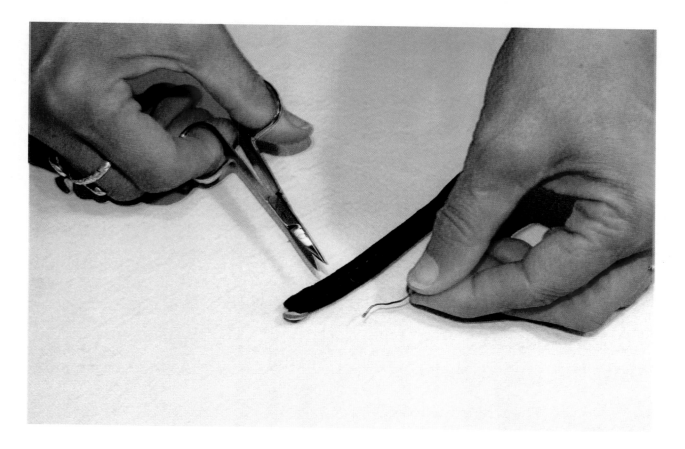

Congratulations! You have just completed your first Saami Inspired Bracelet! It is now time to brandish your bracelet and amaze all of your friends! Stay tuned for upcoming projects and braid variations by joining our blog at **saamsupplies.com** and thank you for purchasing this book.

Chapter - 9

Tips, Tricks and Words of Encouragement

Glue and adhesives
-Remember when gluing down your finished braid on the leather strip apply the glue you choose sparingly. I

prefer rubber cement because it's easy to roll the excess away after it has dried. White craft glue is harder to clean up if you use too much. In the event you do, wet a cotton swab and lightly dab away the excess glue. Remember – you only need the glue as an "assist" to keep your braid straight on the strip while you're stitching. All the glue in the world won't keep the braid on the leather if you don't stitch it properly. *I once glued a braid down so perfectly I mistakenly thought I had already stitched it down to the leather. I donated that bracelet to an art auction and later was informed the winner put on the bracelet and the braid fell off! Luckily I had another ready to replace it.

Invisible (transparent) thread

When using invisible thread you'll need to make a knot big enough to grab the leather without pulling through the puncture made by your first stitch when attaching your pewter braid. Always leave a ¼" tail when making knots with the transparent thread and never trim the tail right up to the knot itself.

Common Threads

For many years I used regular cotton polyester thread to stitch up the back of my bracelets. The preferred

method at present is to use "synthetic sinew" which is really waxed linen fashioned to mimic the use of traditional reindeer sinew. Synthetic
sinew can be purchased by the spool in a "tape" form. You can split the tape into 4-6 single threads for sewing. The advantages I see to using synthetic sinew are two-fold. The wax gives the thread a bit of waterproofing plus the stitches have less of a chance of disintegrating over time. Synthetic sinew also comes in a variety of colors so you can match your leathers with your corresponding shade.

Needles

If you happen to bend your thinner needle in the process of sewing your braid to the leather strip, don't struggle with it. Get a fresh needle and rethread, remembering to make a double knot right up to the eye of the needle. Never use your leather needle to sew your braid to the leather strip. It will cut the pewter thread no matter how careful you think you can be.

Leather

You can use other types of leather besides reindeer hide as long as it is thin enough to take both a thin straight needle and a leather needle. Cow leather, deerskin, pigskin and any kinds of suede leather work well also. I prefer leather with a 1.0mm thickness.

Thimble Use

Using the thinner needle to push through the leather can be hard on the tips of your fingers. If you want to use a thimble there are several options available. A traditional metal thimble works fine for pushing the thinner needles through the leather when you sew your pewter braid to the strip. There are also leather thimbles with small metal plates on them that are more comfortable to use. Go to your local fabric store and check out thimble alternatives too. You can get little "grippy" pads that help you hold on to your needle as well as disposable plastic pads with adhesive that will stick to your preferred thimble finger.

Tools Glorious Tools! Hemostats and Pliers

Having trouble grabbing and pulling your needle once you've pierced the leather? No worries! Using a pair of flat nose pliers, grab the needle and pull it through the leather strip. You can even use a pair of hemostats used to tie flies from the fly fishing store. I've had several awesome nurses as students in my classes who periodically bring me decommissioned hemostats that come in handy for individuals having trouble gripping the needle.

Remember:

I developed many of my techniques by trial and error. Over the years my students have come up with new and innovative ways to improve on a variety of the steps for this project. There are many ways to achieve the same results! Be open to trying or developing ways to make things go more smoothly while you are doing your project. For example, if it feels more comfortable to press the needle down on a hard surface (like a table or plastic cutting board) in order to push it through the leather while you're stitching trust your instincts and do it!

Have fun and stay tuned for future projects! Join our Saami Crafts Facebook page and post your finished projects.

For additional tools, kits and materials, shop www.saamisupplies.com.

Liz Bucheit creates jewelry and body adornment inspired by her Scandinavian ancestry and keeps close ties to her heritage by drawing inspiration from Nordic folklore and myth. A goldsmith for over 30 years, she holds a Master's degree in metalworking and jewelry from the University of Iowa, Iowa City and has trained in traditional jewelry and metalworking techniques in Ireland and Norway. Liz has won numerous competitions and been awarded grants from the Minnesota State Arts Board, McKnight Foundation, Sons of Norway and the SE Minnesota Arts Council. She has exhibited in museums and cultural centers and her bridal tiaras and wedding jewelry are in many collections. Liz is an active speaker on the topic of Norwegian filigree work and conducts workshops and classes in jewelry design and fabrication. She owns and operates Crown Trout Jewelers in Lanesboro, MN.

Made in the USA
Las Vegas, NV
04 November 2023